simplifying **food** and **wine** pairings

Tim Leiwig

authorHOUSE®

AuthorHouse™
1663 Liberty Drive
Bloomington, IN 47403
www.authorhouse.com
Phone: 1-800-839-8640

Published by AuthorHouse 09/16/2014

ISBN: 978-1-4969-3698-1 (sc)
ISBN: 978-1-4969-3697-4 (e)

Library of Congress Control Number: 2014915487

*Any people depicted in stock imagery provided by Thinkstock are models,
and such images are being used for illustrative purposes only.
Certain stock imagery © Thinkstock.*

*Because of the dynamic nature of the Internet, any web addresses or links contained in
this book may have changed since publication and may no longer be valid. The views
expressed in this work are solely those of the author and do not necessarily reflect the
views of the publisher, and the publisher hereby disclaims any responsibility for them.*

CONTENTS

CHAPTER 1

Introduction

Are you intimidated about all of the wine varieties and perhaps what wine will match with what food? Have you been to a restaurant and want to order a glass or bottle of wine for dinner but were unsure and were embarrassed to ask? Or even worse, you ask the wait staff and they can only tell you about the wine varieties that they like, not necessarily that it would complement the food.

Have you been at an important business dinner and because you told your boss you like to drink wine, you were asked to order the wine for dinner?

Wine and food should be fun. Choosing either the wrong food item with the wine you selected or choosing the wrong wine with the food you selected could make either the food or the wine and, in some cases both, taste bad. You might think it was a bad meal or perhaps not a good restaurant. In fact, the problem could have been the pairing. After reading this book and putting what you learn to practice, this will not likely happen to you!

These things happen all of the time. The purpose of this easy to read book is to help you make a decision and be confident that you made a good choice. You will no longer need to feel intimidated or embarrassed. You will be able to ask the necessary questions to get the wine you want, either at a restaurant, wine store or at a social gathering.

While everyone's palate can be different, there are typically distinctive characteristics to each grape varietal (aromas and flavors). I will describe many of the most common grape varieties in a later chapter.

You will be able to use this book, as a reference or guideline, by going to the specific chapter that either interests you or provides you with the information you are seeking. As you saw in the index, chapter 2 will identify basic wine words with a definition. As you learn more about wines you will learn why many of these words (terms) have an impact on the final wine product.

In chapter four, I will provide wine pairings by the grape varietal. While the list will certainly not be all inclusive, you will know what wine to serve with your dinner whether you are hosting an event or going out to a restaurant. You will either be able to provide or order a wine by each course served, or select a wine that matches well with the main course. Of course, do not forget, there are some wonderful wine pairings with appetizers and desserts.

Much of the pairings that are provided have come from meals / food that my wife and I prepared, had at restaurants or gatherings. Not only have I tried many wine and food pairings to see what appears to pair well, I also ask folks all the time about what food and wine pairings they like. Many years have gone into personal research and trial and error to ultimately provide you with what you will find in the pairings chapter. As I mentioned, while you will not find every conceivable food and wine pairing, I believe there are enough possibilities listed that will help you with your pairing decision.

I would also like to add that there are certainly other grape varietals from around the world that are not listed in this book. By no means do I want to suggest that any of the grape varietals not listed are not food friendly. I simply wanted to list wine varietals that you are more likely to see and find readily available. That being said, as you become more familiar with the style and characteristics of the wines you like, part of the fun can be trying a new wine.

Finally, a little about myself ... I have been a long time wine enthusiast. I have been a member of the American Wine Society for many years and I am a past Chapter President. I had been asked to assist in writing a couple of areas for the American Wine Society online wine course. I have visited numerous wineries and met with local restaurant owners and their chef to discuss and recommend wines with their food offerings. I have attended numerous food and wine courses, seminars and trainings and have attempted thousands of probable food and wine pairings/combinations.

While my professional career has been in the public sector; specifically in the Parks & Recreation profession (which I thoroughly enjoy) I have had a long time passion for wine and in particular food and wine pairings.

I believe I have a knack for food and wine pairings. So what do you say ... Let's start your journey!

CHAPTER 2

Basic Wine Terms and Definitions

In this chapter you will find many common and perhaps not so common wine terms. If you have spent any time with others drinking wine, attended a wine tasting or have taken a wine seminar or course, you have likely heard many of the words in this chapter. Each of the words will be briefly described as it is utilized in the wine industry. These definitions will help you better understand what you are hearing and perhaps strengthen your own wine knowledge.

Ah – So – have you ever had a dry cork that began to break or crumple when you tried to open the bottle of wine or have a cork break? The Ah-so is a type of corkscrew with 2 flat metal pieces that can be inserted down the side of the cork. You gently twist or rock back and forth while pulling to remove the cork. You might also hear it called a Butler's Friend.

Alcohol – this word is derived from al kuhl, the Arabic term for a product derived from the process of distillation. It was originally used to manufacture medicines and perfumes. When yeasts consume the sugar in grape juice, you get the alcohol that gives wine a sense of weight on the palate.

Alluvial Fan – several wineries in Napa Valley have vineyards planted in a fan-shaped deposit of soils that have been transported to the site by water. This is known as alluvial fans and they are driven by gravity. Water can be forceful. As such, it made large rocks and soil particles down hillsides or mountains. The water loses momentum as it moves downward depositing

4

finer particles of sand, silt and clay in a fan-shaped pattern on the valley floor.

Anaugebiet (pronounced Ahn Bough Guh Beet) – a major German wine producing region. The anaugebiet can be listed on the German label along with the producer, vintage, grape variety, sweetners level of the wine, village and vineyard where the grapes were grown.

Anthocyanins – the color compounds in grapes belong to a group of plant chemicals known as anthocyanins. This gives wine it's wide array of colors and has been shown to provide antioxidant, anti-cancer and anti-inflammatory properties.

Auvinare – an Italian word. In Italy and in some restaurants in the United States and perhaps elsewhere the wine steward or sommelier will bring the bottle of wine you ordered to your table, along with wine glasses that has a small amount of wine already in one of the glasses. This is called auvinare. Basically the glass is being "primed" for the wine to come. This practice is both considered practical and ceremonial. A glass that has been rinsed with wine is less likely to smell of the dishwashing detergent, chlorinated water or other odors that can collect in the glass. Ceremonially speaking, this practice carries on the spiritual tradition of preparing the vessel (glass) to receive a liquid. In this case, the wine.

This small portion then is transferred throughout each glass at the table. Then the sommelier will pour this wine in his glass and taste to assure the quality of the wine prior to serving.

Balance – balance along with integration are used to describe a good wine. Balance is the characteristic of a wine when the acid, alcohol, fruit and tannins are in balance. Think of how nice a music piece is when everything is in harmony. In integrated wine, the components and flavors have coalesced in a "magical" way. This wine usually will have a unique, singular characteristic.

Barrel Sample – if you have ever been to a winery or plan on going in the future, you will probably have an opportunity to barrel sample or taste, especially if you go on a tour. Here you will be able to taste the wine taken directly from a barrel or a stainless steel tank (tank sample!) or concrete. Please note what you taste as a sample is not likely to be indicative of the final or finished product. Depending on where the wine is in the process when you tasted the sample, the wine is likely to evolve in flavor and the wine maker may utilize techniques or perhaps add another grape variety (blending) to this grape that will definitely change the taste of the wine.

Bitterness – bitterness in food will amplify the bitterness in a wine which could make either the food item or wine or perhaps both taste out of balance. For bitter foods, serve fruity wines.

Bloom – this is when tiny white flowers form on the grapevine. If the temperature is neither too hot nor too cold, the flower will self-pollinate ultimately becoming grapes.

Body – the physical weight of a wine in our mouth is the body. Think of the differences between heavy cream, whole milk and skim or fat-free milk. What body does is tell you a wine's alcohol content (more alcohol means more body).

Bor – you might see this word on a Hungarian wine label. It simply means wine!

Bouchon – A French word meaning stopper. It is typically used to describe a champagne or sparkling wine stopper. It is a metal cap with wings that clamp around the neck of the bottle so the gas does not escape and the bottle goes flat.

Bridge – adding food, spices, herbs or sauces to a dish in order to make that dish better pair with a certain wine or grape variety is considered a bridge. If you want to try to "bridge" a dish, just think about a dominant flavor in the wine you have in mind and add that flavor to the dish.

Brix – this term is used in both the food and wine industries. It is a measurement scale describing the approximate sugar in a wine, fruit juices and soft drinks. For a winemaker, measuring the degrees of Brix reveals the sugar levels in grapes and helps the winemaker decide when to harvest. Brix level can also be used to estimate the approximate alcohol in the final wine. A similar scale in France is called the Baume and in Austria and Germany is known as Oeshsle.

Bud Break – this is part of the season where the grapevines are coming out of dormancy and sprout new growth in the form of tiny green buds. Vintners call this phase of a wines annual lifecycle the "bud break".

Cepage – a French term indicating the percentage of each variety of grape in the composition of a blended wine.

Chalk – this word is often used for limestone. Chalk or limestone soils drain well but are generally not very fertile. This is an asset when it comes to vineyards since many grapevines do best in rather infertile conditions.

Chateau – a chateau is a single estate composed of vineyards surrounding a structure (building) where the wine is made. Chateau is commonly used in Bordeaux, France.

Claret – this is a British term used as a synonym for red Bordeaux wine. The word originated from the French clairet meaning a light red wine. In California this word is now being used for red wines utilizing the grape varieties permissible in Bordeaux. You may also see the term Meritage to indicate a wine has been blended using 2 or more Bordeaux grapes.

Climate – the climate can affect the kinds of wine grown at that particular vineyard or location. Winemakers use three (3) narrower terms for climate:

> Macroclimate – the broad and long term weather patterns in a given geographical area.
> Mesoclimate – the weather patterns in a specific region area (i.e. Carneros region in the Napa Valley)
> Microclimate – the climate in an extremely small defined space such as an area surrounding a few vines.

Clos – a French word meaning an enclosed or walled vineyard. Some American wineries have included the word in their brand names, while the French still use it as part of a vineyard name.

Commune – this French term is used in Burgundy and Bordeaux France. It means a wine village. The practice of referring such villages as communes goes back to the start of the French Revolution. The first commune was Paris. The word commune came from the Latin word communia which means "a small gathering of people sharing a common life".

Concord – concord is the name of the grape variety belonging to the native American grapevine species vitis labrusca. Some is made into wine but it is more often used to make Concord grape juice and Concord grape jelly.

Domaine – a French word generally used in burgundy. It is a collection of vineyard parcels all of which are owned by the same person or entity.

Earthy – many red wines have been described as earthy, such as Bordeaux and Pinot Noir. These "earthy" wines may exhibit one or more of the following characteristics:

- The smell of wild resinous herbs such as thyme or lavender
- The smell of the wet forest floor and rotting leaves
- A mushroom or truffle aroma
- An attractive sensual / sweaty aroma of the human body
- The aroma of animals in a barnyard.

Eleuage – this French term has been used to describe all of the processes of winemaking that occur between fermentation and bottling. This is where the winemaker will decide on what type of barrels to use and how long the wine should remain in them. In other words the decisions that a winemaker makes to reach their final product.

Estate Bottled – an estate bottled wine must come from grapes that are either owned by the winery or under the winery's direct viticultural control through a long term lease. Also, the wine must be completely produced, aged and bottled at the winery. The grapes and winery must be from the same appellation of origin and the appellation must be on the wines label. In Italian wine you will see the phrase imbottigliato allorigine listed on the bottle of an estate wine. The word gutsabfullung is used for estate bottling on German wines and the French say mise enbouteslle au chateau which translates to "bottled at the winery".

Finish – the finish is the lingering flavor of a taste of wine after you swallow. Some folks might consider it the "after taste" of the wine. Wine professionals will tell you that the longer the wine's finish, the better the wine. The longer finish enhances the pleasure you receive from the wine by prolonging the flavors and sensations of the wine.

Frost – frost can result in a significantly smaller crop at harvest. Wineries are also concerned of a frost in the spring especially after the vines begin to have signs of green shoots appearing or when the vines have begun to flower and bear fruit. One method used to minimize or help prevent frost is the use of water over the vine. Sprinklers continuing to spray the vines with water tends not to freeze the vines.

Fungus – one fungus that is known as a friendly fungus is called Botrytis cinerea or often called "noble rot". Some of the most notable wines made using Botrytis are French Sauternes, late harvest German Rieslings and even some American sweet wines. Borytis causes the grapes to shrivel which produces a lot of sugar, honeyed flavors and just enough acid for the wine.

Gamay – a gamay wine has a faint meaty aroma that often comes across with a certain amount of sweetness. Gamay wines also have earthy characteristics such as herbs, stones and the sap in scent of old trees. Some wines from France's Rhone Valley have been described as gamy in a positive manner.

Grip – grip describes a red wine with sufficient tannins to "grip" the palate. Tannins give wine structure. Most top Cabernet Sauvignons and Bordeaux have very good grip.

Gutsabfullung – a German term for estate bottling. (Read more under estate bottling). Erzeugerabfullung means producer bottled. These wines are blended from various vineyards by producers or cooperatives. Both of these terms can be information seen on a German bottle of wine.

Harvest – harvest time at a vineyard can be exciting. There are several factors considered to determine when harvest takes place. One is the sugar content or "brix" level of the grapes (see Brix for more detail). The more sugar a grape contains the more alcohol and body the wine will have. Maturity of other compounds such as tannins and color pigments are also important factors. If grapes are harvested too soon, the wine made from them may be weak in flavor and body. Waiting too long to harvest, there may be a greater risk of heavy rains or frost which could damage the crop as well.

Igneous – igneous rocks are produced by the action of fire. This is an important type of bedrock where vines may grow. Some parts of Napa and Sonoma Valleys are situated on igneous rock.

Lees – lees is an Old English term for the sediment that sinks to the bottle of a container. In wine, the lees are composed mostly of dead yeast cells plus bits of grape skin and seeds that naturally settle out during fermentation in the barrel. Leaving the wine in contact with the lees for an extended period of time causes the wine to take on a creamier mouthful and a richer flavor.

Left Bank – this term refers to all of the appellations of Bordeaux that are on the left side of the Gironde Estuary. The main grape variety grown and used for the Left Bank wines is Cabernet Sauvignon. On the Right Bank wines are mostly made from Merlot and Cabernet Franc.

Legs or Tears – when you swirl a wine in your glass it not only helps aerate the wine but you can see the "legs or tears" on the glass. It is the rivulets of wine that run down the inside of the glass after it is swirled. A wine with "great legs" is generally a wine that is higher in alcohol than one with "poor legs". Legs or tears is not necessarily an indicator as to the quality of the wine.

Limestone – one of the best soils for grapevines is composed of limestone. Limestone is an alkaline sedimentary rock consisting of carbonates. It is porous soil. Some of the most famous limestone-rich soils are in Burgundy, Champagne, South Australia, and New Zealand.

Luscious – many ripe, full bodied wines have been referenced as velvety, smooth, and luscious on the palate. Some folks have also referred to luscious wines as delicious.

Maitre de Chai – this term is commonly used in Bordeaux. A French word for cellar master. The Chai is the place where a chateau's barrels are kept for aging.

Malolactic fermentation – a process that the winemaker uses to make a wine feel smooth on the palate. This process will make a wine seem creamier and buttery. To induce malolactic fermentation, beneficial bacteria are added to the wine. This bacteria will convert the wines tart malic acid to the softer lactic acid.

Meniscus – this is the rim of wine that touches the surface of a wineglass. When drinking a glass of wine, the first step in evaluating a wine is to look at it. Tilt the glass at about a 45 degree angle against a white background under bright or good lighting. This can help you in determining if the wine is "young" or has been aged. For example, if a cabernet sauvignon is young, its deep ruby color will carry through the rim. If the wine has been aged there will be some rim variation. The core of the wine will be deeper in color and the rim "meniscus" will be lighter. In some cases clear or water like or perhaps a little cloudy and white like. Both red and white wines evolve this way over time.

Minerallity or Minerally – many of the world's white wines are described as having a mineral like flavor. Some descriptions include the wine smell and tastes of crushed minerals, stones, wet stones or perhaps the ocean. Some folks use this term to describe a wine that is remarkable in its absence of fruit flavors.

Monopole – this term is used in Burgundy, France for a vineyard with a single owner.

Organic Wines – organic wines are made with grapes grown that follow organic farming principles. This would include not using pesticides, fungicide, herbicides or artificial chemical fertilizers. The specific definition could vary from country to country. One difference of organic wines would be the use of preservatives during the wine making process.

Pinotage – this wine is a signature South African variety. It was developed in the 1920's in South Africa. The southern French grape cinsaut was cross-pollinated with Burgundian Pinot Noir. This is a rustic red wine with aromas of plums or berries. Perhaps you might try a pinotage with barbecue.

Palate – this term is used by winemakers to help describe their wines. A wine that has a prominent front palate tastes intense from the second you taste it. Some wines appear to be more pronounced at the middle palate stage (a few seconds after tasting). Other wines are called back palate wines because they taste moderately intense for several seconds then there is an "explosion" of flavor right before you swallow.

Port – this is the famous fortified wine from Portugal. The name comes from the city of Oporto, a major port city on the Atlantic Ocean north of Lisbon. Port is often poured as an after dinner drink and does well with various desserts. (See pairings the chapter for specific desserts.)

A vintage port is made only in great years when port shippers declare a vintage. The process of declaring a vintage involves approval of the Port Wine Institute. Vintage Port is a blend of grapes (touriga francesa, tinta barroca, tourga nacival and other grapes) from several top wine estates or quintas. Single quinta Ports that come from an estate can be exemplary.

Resveratrol – this is a compound found in red wine and studies have indicated that it may be beneficial to the health of your heart. There are antioxidants in red wine called polyphenols. One of these polyphenols is resveratrol. Red wine has more resveratrol than white wine since the compound is found in grape skins and red wine is fermented with those skins. The skins are removed in white wines before the fermentation process.

Ripasso – this is an Italian term meaning repassed. Ripasso refers to a wine making process where partially dried grape skins are added to a just fermented red wine. Because the skins have some amount of juice, natural sugar and yeast clinging to them, this starts a second fermentation during which the wine takes on more alcohol, body and color.

Saignee – in winemaking this French term refers to a wine made by bleeding off juice from newly crushed grapes before that juice is fermented and before it picks up much color from the grape skins. The saignee process may also be used to increase the intensity of red wines. If some juice is bled from a tank before fermentation, the juice that is left will have greater exposure to the skins, resulting in a more concentrated red wine.

Sommelier (pronounced so-mel-yay) – this is a French term for a wine waiter in a restaurant. It is their job to assist diners in selecting the best wine to match the food dishes selected. A Sommelier can become a Master Sommelier by taking and passing a rigorous exam.

Sonnenuhr – this German word means sundial. Several of Germany's top vineyards are referred to as Sonnenuhr vineyards, and since German wines usually name the vineyard site, you will see the word on the label. During the early Middle Ages, monks carefully positioned a sundial on the hill above a village so it could catch every beam of available light. Its purpose was to determine the exact area on the hill where the snow melted first each year. Over time, the area around the sundial became known as the sundial vineyard and the grapes benefited from the sunny area of which the grapes were planted. These vineyards tend to produce riper and richer wines than other wines grown in the area.

Sourness – sourness in food comes from its natural acids. When a food is high in acidity it can make an accompanying wine taste less acidic. As an example, a pinot grigio or sauvignon blanc will not taste as sour if the food has some acidity.

Super Tuscan – while you are not likely to see these words on a wine label, Super Tuscan is a name bestowed by the media on a certain type of Italian wine. Italy, like many of the European countries, has strict rules governing how wines are made. But in the 1970's some of the Tuscan winemakers were breaking those rules often blending Sangiovese with such French varieties as Cabernet Sauvignon, Cabernet Franc and Merlot. The "power" of these wines moved the wine press to name the style Super Tuscan.

Sweet – In wine the word sweet can mean the actual sweetness derived from sugar or ripeness.

Tastevin – this is a silver, shallow-sided tasting cup. They are usually worn around the neck on a chain. Tastervins were invented centuries ago before wine caves had power. It allowed the winemakers the ability to analyze and taste the wine in the dark cave or cellar. The Tastevin have slight circular indentations (referred to as dimples) in their sides which can reflect candle light across the metal base and make it possible to determine the clarity of the wine drawn from the barrel. At some restaurants the Sommelier or Master Sommelier may be wearing one.

TCA – TCA is a compound that gives wines a smell like a wet dog sitting in a musty basement. This compound is known as 2,4,6 trichloranisole. A wine with TCA is said to be "corked". Humans can detect TCA at a level of five parts per trillion.

Tendril – grapevines grow leaves, grape clusters and a number of tendrils. Tendrils are tiny, slender stems that are branched at their ends. They coil themselves around the trellising vines and help anchor the vines and secure their long leafy arms in an upright position. This helps ensure the leaves don't over shade the grapes. Shaded grapes could produce wine that may taste unpleasant.

Terra Rossa – this term means red earth and is named for the famed soil of the Coonawarra region on South Australia's Limestone Coast. Coonawarra is an Aboriginal word meaning honeysuckle. The entire geologic formation of this region is only 9 miles long and less than three quarters of a mile wide. This region is known for its rich, deep red Cabernet Sauvignon.

Terroir – this French term refers to the sum of all the environmental factors that influence a given vineyard site. All of the environmental factors will influence the way the grape grows, ripens and to some degree how the wine will taste.

Texture – the way the wine feels in your mouth. The textures of wines have been historically described using clothing terms. Examples include: silky, satiny, velvet, soft as cashmere.

Top Off – topping off is a common winemaking practice. After fermentation, many wines spend time in oak barrels. During that time some of the wine evaporates leaving an empty space at the top of the barrel. Since this space of oxygen could possibly spoil the wine, winemakers will regularly top off the barrels with more wine.

Trocken – this is a German term which means dry. When you see this word on a German wine label it means that the wine, by law, has less than 0.9% residual sugar on the palate. A trocken wine is bone dry. Another term, halbtrocken is a half-dry wine. Halbtrocken wines have less than 1.8% residual sugar.

Tropical fruit – this term is often used to describe wines that possess pineapple, mango, guava and papaya aromas and flavors. These will most likely be white wines made from grapes grown in warm climates.

Typicity or typicality – is often one of the most important barometers by which old world wines are judged. As an example, in order for a wine to be labeled Bordeaux or Chianti, the French or Italian vintner, respectively must submit their wine to a panel of judges who, by tasting it, will determine whether or not its flavor is typical of that region.

Umami – umami is a Japanese word which has gained acceptance in the scientific community as the fifth taste. It means deliciousness or savoriness. Foods high in umami share a concentration of glutamates which can magnify the flavor of the food. Examples include most meats, Parmesan cheese, many concentrated sauces, lobster and many cheeses. Umami foods can make a wine taste metallic or bitter. Foods high in umami taste best with wines that have a rich core of fruit.

Unfiltered – wines that are unfiltered have not received any of the filtration methods that separate the wine from microscopic organisms such as bacteria and yeasts. Most winemakers worldwide filter their wines to some degree. The key is to know how much to filter so as not to completely strip the wine of its character and flavor.

Unoaked – a term typically seen on white wine labels. Unoaked refers to a wine that was not made or aged in barrels. As an example many chardonnays are made unoaked. These wines are often made in stainless steel tanks. An unoaked chardonnay typically tastes fresher, more crisp and fruity with apple and pear like notes.

Variety, Varietal – the variety refers to a type of grape. A varietal is a type of wine.

Veraison – in the early summer to midseason, grapes form as tiny green beads begin to set, swell and grow. Once the grapes nearly reach full size, color compounds within the grapes begin to develop. This causes the grapes to change color. This process is known as veraison. It signals the grapes final push to full ripening. Veraison typically occurs in August and/or September in the Northern Hemisphere, depending on the specific grape variety and climate conditions.

Vintage – a vintage is based on the year the grapes were picked, not the date the wine was released. Vintage dates were historically provided to inform the consumer the age of any given wine. This is especially important for white wines since many are often preferred young and fresh. A vintage date may also allow the wine drinker to form a preliminary idea or opinion of what the wine may be like.

V.O.S and V.O.R.S. – the finest Sherrys count among the most extraordinary wines of the world. The sherry label V.O.S. stands for Vinum Optimum Signatum or Very Old Sherry. To qualify as V.O.S., a sherry must have been aged in barrels for a minimum of twenty years. V.O.R.S. stands for

Vinum Optimum Rare Signatum or Very Old Rare Sherry. These must be aged for a minimum of thirty years in barrels and are produced in tiny quantities.

Yeast – yeasts are microscopic single-cell organisms responsible for converting sugar alcohol. There are many different strains of yeast. French chemist Louis Pasteur discovered the role of yeasts in winemaking more than a century and a half ago. This discovery "rocked" the scientific world.

CHAPTER 3

Wine Characteristics, Aromas, and Flavors

In this chapter I am going to present some typical characteristics, aromas, and flavors in each grape variety. Along with this information, I will list various food items that will pair with the wine. When you are at a restaurant, preparing for a social gathering, party or simply wanting a glass of wine with a snack, this chapter will guide you.

Let me begin by stating that this book/guide will not list every grape variety or blend that is available around the world. It will list, however, many of the grape varieties that you are likely to see in a restaurant or purchase for yourself or as a gift.

Distinctive Aromas and Tastes of Wines

Champagne / Sparkling wine: Bubbles, pear, fresh bread dough (see more details in chapter 5).

White wines:

Arneis: Aromas of almonds, apricots, peaches, pears and hops. Characteristics of pears, apple, licorice grapefruit, white flower with medium acidity.

Bordeaux Blanc: aromas of grapefruit and pears. Flavors of strawberry, raspberry or cherry.

Chenin Blanc: Minerally, angelica, green, honey, chalky, apple.

Chardonnay: Flavors such as smoke, creamy, cloves, caramel, spice, coconut, cinnamon, vanilla. Neutral taste with hints of minerals and green apples or buttered baked apples, almonds, tropical fruit and custard.

Gavi: aromas of citrus, fruit and minerals.

Gewurzteminer: Lychees, roses, floral notes and passion fruit

Pinot Gris / Pinot Grigio: flora, pears, apple and melon

Riesling: a petrol note, kerosene, rubber, flower, tropical fruits and mineral stone

Nice balance of fruit and acid, although Riesling can span both ends from dry to sweet.

Sauvignon Blanc: grass, herbs, lemon, green, grapefruit or hay. Powerful with the smell of the outdoors.

New Zealand Sauvignon Blanc: aromas and flavors of citrus fruit, herbal and hints of grassiness, lemon and gooseberries.

Voigner: floral aromas, fruit forward, aromatic

White Burgundy: aromas of peaches, apples and citrus. Young wines will have aromas of fern, mint or tobacco. The higher end wines will display notes of rose, chamomile, hawthorn, honeysuckle, verbena and possible hints of oak.

White Zinfandel: aromas of raspberry and blackberries.

Red Wines:

Amarone: the more traditional style tends to have aromas and flavors of plums, black cherry and dried fruit. The modern style has aromas of dried fruit and toasted oak. There may be notes of coconut or vanilla.

Beaujolais: Typically a fruity easy to drink wine. Flavors of ripe red fruit.

Bordeaux: aromas and flavors of dark cherry, casis, blackberry, black cherry, vanilla, coffee bean, spice, licorice, truffles, tobacco, leaf, tar, leather or forest floor.

Cabernet Franc: aromas of tobacco, raspberry, bell pepper, cassis, violets, peppery, graphite and black currant, green leaves. This grape is often used for blending.

Cabernet Sauvignon: notes of herbaceous, green bell pepper, flavors of mint and eucalyptus, black current and tobacco, vanilla, spice, smell of blackberry, blueberry, sage and tobacco. High tannins. Flavored from the use of oak.

Chianti: aromas of cherry, nutty and perhaps floral notes.

Malbec: aromas of tobacco, raisin, blackberry and violet aromas.

Grenache: notes of raspberries, strawberries, black olives, coffee, gingerbread, honey, spices, tar, and black currant.

Merlot: notes of casis, black & red cherries, black tea, fennel, oregano, blueberry, boysenberry, mulberry, plum, black and green olives, cola nut

Mourvede: intense fruit flavors and notes of black bean, gamy or meaty flavors. As it ages more earthy, leather and gingerbread.

Nebbiolo: tar, roses, dried fruit, leather, licorice, mulberries, spice and dried and fresh herbs, truffles, tobacco and prunes.

Pinot Noir: aromas of black and red cherries, raspberry and currant, cherry cola, strawberries, truffles and earth. Very food friendly.

Rioja: the aromas and flavors can differ based upon the blend of grapes. The red Riojas tend to have fruit aromas with possible spice, earth, chocolate and oak notes.

Sangiovese: black cherry, black currant, mulberry, plum

Super Tuscan: can be highly aromatic and have violet and cedar characteristics. Flavors of chocolate, tobacco and mint.

Syrah/Shiraz: violets, dark berries, chocolate, espresso, black pepper, blackberries, smoky & spicy characteristics.

Tempranillo: aromas and flavors of plum, herbs, tobacco, strawberry and vanilla.

Zinfandel: aromas of berry, raspberry and sometimes spice and pepper. Flavors include dark berry, raspberry, licorice and slight spice pepper. Some consider this grape varietal to be "jammy" (very fruit forward and drier).

CHAPTER 4

Food and Wine Pairings

In this chapter you will find more common grape varieties listed. Under each grape varietal you will find the food items that will pair with that particular grape. If you are at a restaurant and see what you are going to order, check this reference list to see which wine or wines will pair with the dish. Remember that the sauces and/or spices could potentially change the wine you choose. That is why many of the food items listed in this chapter are specific.

Summer grilling

With light appetizers, cheese or seafood, grilled shrimp, light chicken with olive oil (not lemon or vinegar)

> Pinot Gris (Pinot Grigio)
> Sparkling wine or champagne

With grilled dishes

> Pinot Noir
> Cabernet Franc
> Cabernet Sauvignon
> Zinfandel

Light Bodied Whites

Pinot Grigio (Pinot Gris), Arneis, Sauvignon Blanc

White bean dip
Unsalted Cape Cod potato chips
Goat cheese
Sushi / California roll
Roasted red peppers
Veggies & dip
Garlic bread with basil pesto
Boursin cheese
Gouda cheese

Salty food: High acid, somewhat sweet wines

Salt cancels the sugar in wine so stick with the more fruity wine (or fruit forward red wine) dry Riesling, Pinot Grigio (Pinot Gris) or Riesling, see examples below:

Sushi/sashimi   Dry Riesling
Stir fry   Pinot Grigio (Pinot Gris) or Reisling
Salted Nuts   Zinfandel

Tart food: Lightly sweet fruity wines
Tart food negate fruitiness in wine. Examples to consider include Beaujolais, some Pinot Noirs, Gewurtzraminer, Gruner Veltliner, Viognier

Spicy foods: Lightly sweet, fruity, low-tannin wines
Spicy food can also cancel fruit, so avoid the tannins. Thai foods tend to compliment wines with residual sugar or a lot of fruit and acidity.

Fish: Full bodied, high acid, medium-bodied wines
Wine can overwhelm many fish unless they are served with a fruit salsa or garnish. A bland fish, like poached sole with sautéed spinach, needs a delicate slightly sweet wine such as a Pinot Grigio (Pinot Gris) or

Sauvignon Blanc. Meanwhile an oily fish, like salmon, especially when grilled is perfectly paired with a Pinot Noir.

Game: Big reds
The tannins in bold reds balance flavorful meats, especially barbecue.

Rich dishes: Full flavored, high acid wines
Rich needs rich. A grilled, stilton-stuffed filet mignon topped with hollandaise and crabmeat simply begs for a big, full-flavored red wine or Chardonnay.

Smoked foods: Low-tannin, very rich and/or somewhat sweet wines
Few wines can match the taste overload of smoked foods. Only the strongest wines will be left standing. Keep in mind if the dish is smoked fish or smoked duck, the sauce and other factors. The type of sauce and other factors could cause the item to be the dominant flavor of the dish. Choose your wine accordingly.

Grilled foods: Big reds or big whites
Anything grilled, even shrimp or lobster, moves up a notch from a light-bodied flavor to a medium or high full bodied flavor. Adjust your wine as needed.

If a dish is made with a wine reduction or wine sauce, ask what wine or grape varietal was used and order it with your meal or dessert.

Sparkling / Champagne

Most seafood	Lobster bisque
Caviar	Smoked salmon
Crème brulee	Smoked and blackened foods
Sushi rolls	Most anything salty
Fruit	Hummus with chips, pita or vegetables
Bruschetta (tomato based)	Salsa
Light chicken dishes	Potato chips
Grilled salmon	Salads with fruit (strawberries, melon, apple, mandarin orange)
Popcorn	Honey roasted pecans

Cheese

Camembert	Edan
Brie	Boursin
Chevre	Colby
Mild cheddar	

Arneis

White bean dip	Shrimp cocktail
Tomato salsa or Bruschetta	Sushi or California rolls
Teriyaki chicken	Dips and spreads with sundried tomato

Cheese

Goat	Feta

Bourdeax Blanc

Seasonal vegetable soup	Duck
Scallops wrapped in bacon	Shrimp scampi
Grilled shrimp	Cheese Fondue

Chardonnay

Roasted lobster with verjus and tarragon	Grouper with collard greens
Tortilla soup	Pasta in a cream sauce
Light Asian vegetable dishes	Chicken
Turkey	Potato latkes
Sliced avocado	Grilled shrimp
Shrimp scampi	Fish / shellfish chowder

Chardonnay, continued

Fatty fish	Cream soups
Vegetable side dishes	Baba ganoush
Salmon club sandwiches	Grilled scallops with honeydew and avocado salsa
Rich fish dishes	Fish curry
Slow roasted pork belly	Oysters
Salmon	Veal cutlets
Crab dishes	Lobster bisque
Halibut	Corn soup
Garlic dips	Sliced avocado
Chicken salad	Cashews, pistachios
Salmon and avocado salad	

Cheese

Baked brie	Camembert
Mild cheddar	Cheese fondue
Rich creamy cheeses	Bucheron

Chenin Blanc

Chicken Teriyaki	Shellfish
Smoked Salmon	Asian dishes
Grilled shrimp	Light fish dishes
Grilled fish	Citrus influenced and vegetable stir fry

Cheese

Camembert	Bleu
Monterey Jack	Colby
Derby	

Gavi

Crab dip	Shrimp Scampi
Grilled shrimp	Simple seafood dishes
Tomato dishes	Linguine in pesto sauce

Cheese

Asiago	Parmesean

Gewurtaminer

Curry	Sweet and sour dishes
Dishes with lots of fresh herbs	Chicken
Turkey	Beijing burgers
Thai curry soup	Ham
Stir-fried vegetables	Sausage
Spicy Asian foods	Foie Gras
Goose	Sweet and spicy dishes
Spicy hot Italian sausage	Smoked salmon
Moroccan style chicken	Brazilian chicken curry

Cheese

Gruyer	Bleu
Aged cheddar	Meunster
Boursin	Chevre
Jarlsberg	Swiss
Alpine Shepard Durus	

Pinot Grigio / Pinot Gris

Smoked and blackened foods	Tomatoes
Salsa or Bruschetta topping	3 nut turkey burgers with tropical salsa
Guacamole	Shrimp cocktail
Light fish dishes	Veggies and dip
Dips and spreads with sundried tomato	Lobster
Venison	Artichokes
Chicken and apple sausage	Vegetable pizza – grilled
Liver pate	Foie Gras
Chicken with olive oil	Chicken with lemon & capers
Vegetables	California roll
White bean dip	Teriyaki chicken

Cheese

Goat	Feta
Danish bleu	Havarti
Asiago Fresco or baked	Mozzarella
Jarlsberg	

Melon

Riesling (Dry)

Sweet and Spicy foods	Fish pate
Crab dishes	Melons
Glazed ham	Guacomole
Asian foods	Smoked and blackened foods
Chicken	Turkey
Foie Gras	Fresh or smoked bratwurst
Asparagus	Shrimp cocktail
Indian dishes	Lobster
Oysters	Pork
Asian dishes	Simple Mexican dishes

Cheese

Goat milk cheese	Emmental
Colby	Gouda
Havarti	Monterey Jack
Swiss mountain cheese	Edam
Cheshoe cheese	

White Chocolate with a Riesling Ice Wine / Candied Walnuts

Sauvignon Blanc

Glazed ham	Sushi or California rolls
Tart dressing and sauces	Chicken or fish with lemon
Artichokes	Grilled shrimp
Smoked salmon	Grilled fish
Oysters	Salmon burgers with lemon cilantro mayonnaise
Phyllo pizza with feta and basil	Crab cakes
Beats, goat cheese and avocado salad	Spicy hot Italian sausage
Greek salad with feta cheese & black olives	Asparagus
Roasted red peppers	Asian egg rolls
Mussels	

Cheese

Bousin	Goat
Feta	Sharp cheddar
Chevre	Brie
Chesire	

New Zealand Sauvignon Blanc

Vegetable dip	Melon
Spicy foods	Guacamole
Light appetizers	Teriyaki chicken
Tart dressings and sauces	Chicken or fish with lemon
Grilled fish	Smoked salmon

Viognier

Duck frittes	Indian tandoori dishes
French toutouse sausage	Fried chicken
Southeast Asian foods	Spicy foods
Shrimp scampi	Grilled shrimp

Cheese

Ripe cheeses	Goat
Light bleu	Monterrey Jack
Gouda	

Vouvray

Sweet and spicy dishes	Asian or Indian dishes
Basic seafood dishes and shellfish	

Cheese

Chevre	Camembert
Blue	

White Burgundy (French Chardonnay)

Pasta, white cream sauce	Shellfish
Boudin blanc (sausage)	Garlic sauces

Cheese

Brie	

White Zinfandel

Tomato based dishes	Teriyaki
Honey mustard	

Rosé

Garlic dishes	Grilled chicken
Light appetizers	Watermelon salad
Shellfish dishes	scallops
Smokey eggplant and fresh tomatoes	Rich cheesy dishes
Light fish dishes	Shrimp gumbo
Ratatouille	

Appetizer: smoked salmon; chicken; canapes

Entrée: grilled salmon; poultry

Dessert: berry tart; fresh berries

Amarone

Braised and roasted meats	Dishes with rich meat sauces
Stews	Roasted game
Pumpkin risotto	Venetian dishes
Tomato and truffle sauces	

Cheese

Aged cheeses	

Beaujolias
Meat:

Roast turkey	Chicken livers wrapped in bacon
Chicken Stew	Beef
French Toulouse Sausage	Teriyaki chicken / beef
Liver pate	Pork
Cod	

Cheese

Havarti	Gouda
Charo Lais	Dubliner Irish
Boursin	Aged Cheddar
Brie	Asiago

Vegetables/Fruit

Fresh Fruit	Sweet Potatoes
Baked stuffed mushrooms	Hummus
Brussel sprouts	

Dark Chocolate

Bordeaux

Dishes flavored with green peppers and mushrooms	Grilled beef
Chinese spare ribs	Filet of beef with liver pate
Steak	Béarnaise sauce
Rack of lamb	Buffalo burgers
Beef ribs	

Cheese

Aged cheddar	Havarti
Hard Pyrenees	Spanish Mountain
Colby	Roquefort
Camembert	

Bittersweet dark chocolate

Cabernet Franc

Lamb	Steak
Sweet / spicy BBQ sauces	Tomme de Savoie cheese
Indian food with little to no heat	Hearty dishes in a red sauce

Cabernet Sauvignon*

Olive tapenade	Marinated skirt steak on a crostini
Sweet potato	Beef tenderloin
Roast beef	Beef teriyaki
Roast lamb	Duck
Goose	Pepper crusted Ahi tuna
Chinese spare ribs	Buttered pecans
Buffalo burgers with herbs	Toasted walnuts
Dishes that include the oak influenced flavors and aromas	Dishes spiced with vanilla, brown sugar, nutmeg and dill weed
Indian food with little to no heat	Grilling methods such as grilling, charring, smoking or plank roasting
Prime rib	Steaks
Venison	Juicy red meats
Lamb chops with herbs	Beef ribs
Short ribs braised in red wine (Cab)	Dishes flavored with green pepper and mushrooms

Cheese

Colby cheese	Cheddar
Mozzarella	Sharp Cheddar

Cabernet Sauvignon* continued

San Andreas	Pecorino Romano
Brie	Goat
Hard Pyrenees	Danish bleu
Camembert	Monterey Jack
Carmody cheese	Aged Gouda
Le Moulis	

* As the wine ages, the tannins will soften then more subtle and less bitter dishes will be a better match.   Desserts made primarily with bitter dark chocolate.

Chianti

Italian cuisine	Beef tenderloin
Artichokes	Lamb
Mild Italian sausage	Salmon (smoked or regular)
Bacon	Creamed mushroom bruschetta
Pizza	Tomato dishes
Dishes in red sauces	Minestrone

Cheese

Pecorino Romano	Provolone
Swiss	Gouda
Parmesan	Pecorino Toscano

Grenache

Creamed mushroom bruschetta	Liver Pate
Baked stuffed mushrooms	Sausage (not too spicy)
Non-salty ham	Smoked Salmon
Salmon	

Cheese

Swiss	Gouda
Havarti	

Malbec

Hams with sweet – spicy barbeque sauce	Blood sausage
Steak	BBQ Beef Ribs
BBQ Chicken	Foods with sweet / spicy BBQ sauces
Tri-tip Salad	

Cheese

Aged Cheddar	Dubliner Irish
Iberico	Taleggio
Cashel Blue	Manchego

Merlot

Salmon	Roast turkey
Beef tenderloin	Roast lamb
Sauerkraut	Game birds
Meatloaf	Burgers
Eggplant roasted in chimichuri sauce	Toasted walnuts
Beef	Mushrooms

- Salmon, Chard & Radicchio for softer and fruitier Merlot
- Shellfish especially wrapped in bacon or prosciutto – for Light-bodied Merlot
- Robust meats for the more full-bodied Merlot

Cheese

Aged Monterey Jack	Alpine Shepard
Gruyere	Gouda
Camembert	Blue veined cheeses

Dark chocolate (example 70% cocoa)

Nebbiolo

Mild Italian sausage	

Cheese

Fontina	Prave
Grana Padano	Gorgonzola
Roquefort	Sharp Cheddar

Petite Sirah

Merguez sausage	Lamb
Chilean-infused sausage such as Mexican Chorizo or chicken and turkey habanero	Roast turkey
Venison	Roast duck
Grilled Steak	Jerk Chicken

Cheese

Hard French mountain cheese	Gouda
Arina	Benning
Saint-Florentin	

Pinot Noir
Meats:

Smoked or roast turkey	Smoked pig
Lamb & beet root	Duck
Goose	Teriyaki chicken or beef
Grilled or seared tuna	Smoked bratwurst
Duck sausage	Salmon
Bacon	Sage flavored pork sausage
Garlic grilled pork tenderloin	Chicken

Pinot Noir, continued

Smoked and blackened foods	Arctic Char
Crab dishes	Earthy flavored dishes
Sushi	Salmon burger

Vegetables / Fruit

Portobello burgers	Stuffed onions with almonds and parmesan
Grilled vegetables	Artichokes
Gazpacho	Wild mushroom risotto
Hummus	Strawberries
Smoked almonds	Baked stuffed mushrooms
	Truffles

Cheese

Brie	Camembert
Provolone	Asiago
Gouda	Swiss
Jarlsberg	Cheddar (light)
Edam	Gruyere
French Chevre	

Red Burgundy

Duck	Charbroiled chicken
Sushi	Mushrooms
Turkey	

Cheese

Camembert	

Rhone Varietals

Meat with herb crusts or sauces	Lamb
Truffles	Roast duck
Merguez sausage	Chicken Kiev
Roast turkey	Venison
Game birds	Sweet / spicy BBQ Sauce
Tri-tip salad	Asian BBQ

Cheese

Gruyere	Camembert
Reblochon	

Rioja Region (Spanish Red)

Fish stews	Sautéed Mushrooms or Mushrooms
Lamb	Risotto
Pork	Beef
Paella	Charbroiled Meats

Cheese

Makon	Idiazabal
Garrotxa	Tetilla

Sangiovese

Herbed potato croquette with roasted red tomatoes	Italian tomato based dishes
Toasted walnuts	Pizza
Lasagna	Calzones
Pasta with red sauce	Herbed potato croquette with roasted red tomatoes

Cheese

Ricotta	Provolone
Pecorino	Fontina
Parmesan Reggiano	Asiago
Mozzarella	

Super Tuscan

Hearty Italian dishes with red sauce	Chicken Cacciatore
Veal Parmesan	Portobello Mushrooms
Venison	Grilled Steak
Salomi, prosciutto	Lamb Chops
Osso buco (braised veal)	Herb rubbed pork roast

Cheese

Parmigano Reggiuno	Pecorino Romano

Syrah / Shiraz

Smoked almonds	Merguez sausage
Spicy ethnic foods such as Indian or Mexican	Game Birds
Roast Lamb	Beef
Duck	Chipotle Honey BBQ Bacon Burgers
Shepard's pie (beef)	Goose
Veal	Ribeye steak with bleu cheese sauce
Beef Teriyaki	Grilled beef
Barbeque and grilled meats	Meatballs
Buffalo	Beef Brisket
Elk and Kangaroo	Beef short ribs
Meat casseroles	Burgoo (stew)

Cheese

Cheddar	Edam
Gouda	Gruyere
Hard French mountain cheese	St. Nectaire

Tempranillo

Mixed grilled vegetables	Paella
Meatballs	Tapas
Portobello Mushrooms	Grilled meats

Cheese

Sharp Cheddar	Havarti
Manchego	Tomme de Savole
Mahon	Azeitao

Zinfandel

Roast turkey	Beef tenderloin
Sausage stuffing	Mild Italian sausage
Spicy sage and red pepper country sausage	Pates, mousses, terrines
Grilled spice rubbed pork	Chili
Buffalo wings	Chorizo sausage
Rustic and rich dishes	Comfort foods
BBQ Beef brisket	BBQ Chicken
Tacos	Pizza
Buffalo wings	Grilled sausages with peppers
Buffalo	Creamy chicken liver mousse
Hamburger	

Cheese

Bleu	Colby
Sharp Cheddar	Parmigiano-Reggiano
Stilton	Gouda
Asiago	Gruyere
Dry Sonoma Jack	Meunster
Goat cheese	

Maderia

Pumpkin pie	Dark chocolate
Tiramisu	

Mourvedre

Meat based stews	Lamb dishes
Spicy Paella	Turkey burger

Port

Dark Chocolate	

Cheese

Stilton	Bleu

White Port:

Appetizer: Fresh melon; smoked ham

Entrée: Smoked salmon

Dessert: dark chocolate

Tawny Port

Almond tart	Dark chocolate
Toffee caramel cake	Pecan pie
Smoked almonds	Foir Gras pate
Red fruits	Milk chocolate with nuts
Crème brulee	Pretzels

Cheese

Stilton	Bleu

Ruby Port

If cheese is served as a dessert, serve bleu cheese, cheddar with Reserve Ruby Port. Also dark chocolate and red fruits pair well.

Sauternes

Apple pie	Shortbread
Sugar cookies	Pear or apple tart
Foie Gras	

Cheese

Bleu	Roquefort
Crème Brulee	

become very popular as an aperitif due to their light, dry taste. They are also ideal for light first courses including seafood, soups and salads.

<u>Blanc de Noir</u>: This is a Champagne or sparkling wine made from Pinot Noir and/or Meunier grapes. Typically these wines are full bodied and deeper yellow-gold in color. They are ideal for full flavored foods including meats and cheeses.

<u>Pink or Rosé</u>: Rosé Champagne or sparkling wines are made utilizing one of two methods. The first method involves adding a small amount of red still wine to the original blend. The second method involves exposing the must to the skins of the grape when pressing.

<u>Non- Vintage or NV</u>: With Champagne, a non-vintage is a wine composed of several different years and different blends as well as different vintages, rather than from a single harvest.

<u>Vintage</u>: All grapes used have been harvested from a single year.

<u>Cuvee de prestige</u> These are made from blends of the most subtle wines. In Champagne many of these wines are going to be a top-end Champagne. They may or may not be vintage and are typically aged for an extended period of time.

As I mentioned earlier, if a sparkling wine is made any other place in the world, outside of the Champagne region of France, the Champagne term cannot be used. So again, outside of the Champagne region, France refers to their sparkling wines as cremant. Some Sparkling wines from other countries you are likely to see or perhaps have tried include:

Cava, from Spain
Procecco and Moscato d'Asti, from Italy
Sekt, from Germany
Penina, from Slovenia
Sparkling Shiraz, from Australia

You might read on the bottle that the sparkling wine was made utilizing the traditional method (method tradionelle). This is simply that it was made following the method in Champagne. In a chapter 4 you will see a list of food items that will pair well with Champagne and sparkling wines.

Let's talk a little about sparkling wines and Champagne aromas and flavors. Sometimes, due to the bubble sensation in your mouth, it may be difficult to describe anything else.

Listed below are words used to describe Champagne and sparkling wine. See if you might find a few of these flavors with the next Champagne or sparkling wine you try.

Orange/orange peel	Fresh bread dough	Minerals	Damp Soil
Tangerine	Brioche	Mushroom	Quince
Pear	Toasted bread	Stones	Apple
Pineapple	Yeast	Earth	Coconut
Vanilla	Grapefruit	Honey	Rose pedals
Spices	Toffee	Cream soda	Ginger
Caramel	Butter	Marzipan	Grilled Nuts
Lemon	Lemon meringue pie		

Champagne and sparkling wines are often offered at celebrations and events. But they are very versatile and food friendly. Therefore do not be afraid to order a bottle or open a bottle anytime. In chapter 6 we will be discussing hosting a social event or party. Having an event around Champagne and sparkling wines can be fun. As I mentioned, they are food friendly. Everyone can bring their favorite Champagne or sparkling wine to share and there is a lot of information to discuss with folks about these wines. Make it fun and at the same time folks may learn something new or helpful.

For example, you might ask guests if they know what the wine cage that holds the Champagne or sparkling wine cork to the neck of the bottle is called. The answer is a muzzle or muselet. Another question might be … in a Champagne or sparkling wine producer's cellar there are people in the cellar constantly turning the bottles. What are they called? The answer is riddlers (English); reurveurs (French). Another question could be what is the French term for "stopper" which is typically used to describe a Champagne or sparkling wine stopper. The answer is bouchon. Finally, to find out who really is knowledgeable about Champagne or sparkling wines, you might ask; how many bottles of sparkling wine will one grapevine produce each year? The answer is only four or five bottles.

They may also be used to make various cocktails such as Kir Royale, Bellini, Mimosa or Ocean Breeze.

Champagne / Sparkling

Champagne can be served as an aperitif and can also be served with appetizers, entrees and desserts.

Non-Vintage:

Appetizer: Sushi rolls; oysters
Salad: Spinach salad with red onions and strawberries or oranges
Entrée: Grilled fish; scallops; Asian cuisine
Dessert: on its own

Vintage:

Appetizer: light canapes
Entrees: game; roast lamb; fish

(See chapter 4 for more wine and food parings with Champagne and Sparkling wines.

Match each sparkling wine with its native country:

1.	Prosecco	A.	Germany
2.	CAVA	B.	Italy
3.	Cremant	C.	Spain
4.	Sekt	D.	France

bridge. As you may recall, from the terms and definition chapter, you could bridge food with spices and/or sauces added to a dish in order for that dish to "work" with a particular wine. Just think about a dominant flavor in the wine, and then add that flavor to the dish. Again, you can refer to chapter 3 to review typical characteristics, aromas and flavors of each grape variety.

Another option for a dinner may be a pairings dinner. Here, if your guests like wine as well, you develop a menu – appetizers, soup/salad, main course and dessert (as an example) and pair wines with each course. You may ask your guests to select a course and make it to feed the number of total guests expected to come to the dinner. They would bring along a bottle of wine that would pair with the food course. Remember, if your guests are not confident in selecting wines that pair with the food, they might look to you for advice for what wine to bring. Of course, you can refer to this book/guide to help provide them an answer! In any case, everyone is learning and at the same time it takes out much of the anxiety from selecting the "right" wine. Either way, let me suggest you purchase a 1 or 2 ounce wine pourer. This will allow each guest to taste the wine with the intended course and depending on how many guests you have, may allow guests to go back to taste the wine later in the evening or perhaps with another course. This allows sufficient wine to taste with the food item and cuts down on the overall number of bottles needed for each course and the entire dinner.

This would be a good time to discuss how many ounces you would receive in a typical 750 ml wine bottle. Each bottle has a total of 25.4 ounces. This would inform you or your guests on how many bottles will be needed based on the size of the pour and number of guests.

> 2 ounces pours would serve 12 people
> 3 ounce pours would serve 8 people
> 4 ounce pours would serve 6 people
> 5 ounce pours would serve 5 people
> 6 ounce pours would serve 4 people

Remember that fruits and some ingredients, such as many barbecue sauces and teriyaki sauces add sweetness to a dish. Caramelization that comes from roasting, grilling or sautéing can also contribute to the sweetness of a dish. Sweeter food will decrease the perception of the sweetness of a wine. If the food has some sweetness, choose a wine that has a degree of sweetness as well. If the desert is very sweet, serve a dessert wine that is even sweeter.

Perhaps you are just interested in hosting a wine tasting. With your new found knowledge of wine, why not?

Let me provide you with some basic information that will allow you to host a wine tasting for your friends and family that is sure to be fun and informative.

Hosting a wine tasting

If you plan on tasting both red and white wines, it is best to begin with the white wines. Start with the drier white wines and progress towards the sweeter whites. In some cases, you might find it better when tasting white wines to start with the sweetest and work towards the dry. While it is certainly your preference, I prefer the latter. To me, my palate is better prepared to move to the red wines if I finish with a dry white. Of course, it is a good idea to have some unsalted crackers or neutral food to help cleanse the palate between wines.

When you are ready to taste the red wines, start with the light body reds and move towards the heavier body wines.

Ask your guests about the "bouquet or nose" of each wine. This refers to what the wine smells like. If someone says the scent is like toast or fresh bread, they are likely describing a yeast or fresh dough scent. They could also be referring to the toasted oak that comes from the barrels where many wines are kept when processing. Your guests might describe the scent as minerally. This refers to a wine that is reminiscent of wet stone or flint. They might also refer to the wine as herbal. Refer back to chapter 3 describing each wine for more detail on characteristics, aromas and flavors focused in each grape variety. Also see chapter 4 for suggested pairings. I will list typical flavors and scents found in a few wines below:

Chardonnay – apple, pear
Sauvignon Blanc – grass and herbs
Pinot Noir – ripe cherries, strawberry, earthy
Merlot – cherry, red fruit
Petite Sirah – plum and spice
Cabernet Sauvignon – black current, dark fruits

Serving Temperatures:
Sparkling /Champagne: 40 - 46 degrees
Whites: 46 - 52 degrees
Rose and Late harvest: 46 -52
Reds: 58 - 65 degrees

Now you are ready to pour the first wine to your guests. Have them swirl the wine in the glass (not recommended for Champagne or sparkling wines). This will help release the aromas and allow the wines to breath. Then have your guests bring their nose to the glass and ask them to breath in the aromas.

When you sniff a wine look for these common notes:

Herbs and spices: Tobacco, mint, thyme, black pepper, clove, fennel
Wood: Smoke, tree bark, tar, eucalyptus, cedar
Fruit: Plum, cherry, blueberry, raspberry, blackberry, fig, coconut, watermelon, orange, pomegranate, peach, apple, lemon
Vegetable: Black olive, beet, green bean, baked potato, rhubarb, bell pepper
Floral: Violet, rose, lavender, lilac, honeysuckle, orange
Earth: Underbrush, mushrooms, truffles, soil

The next step is to sip the wine. Allow air to enter into your mouth. The air will mix with the wine and release extra flavors. Allow the wine to roll around in your mouth before swallowing. If you want to make this more of a learning experience, provide pencils and paper to allow each guest to record their observations of each wine they taste. This may further enhance their wine experience and perhaps provide information on wines of which they have interest to purchase. Finally have a wine bucket handy. Since it is possible that your guests may not like all of the wines, the bucket can be used to allow your guest to pour out the remainder of the wine that they dislike.

Hosting a wine event

Hosting a wine or food and wine event can be fun. It is a great way to continue to explore and learn about wines as well as food pairings. Ideas for hosting an event:

- Viva Las Vegas: Do a blind tasting with characteristics of wine that match your favorite game – black jack, roulette, craps, poker.
- Bottles with pretty labels
- Wines from a specific country or region
- Wines from the country of your ancestry
- A progressive food and wine event: if your guests live close by, you could consider a progressive food and wine event. Have each course of the dinner with the accompanying wine would be held at each of the guests home or you could have 1-2 courses at one house and the remainder (main course / dessert) at another home.
- Wine Trivia Event – Have questions for guests to answer about wines. You will find many items in this book to create your own questions. See chapter 5 for a few example questions.
- Themed events around the holidays, soups, summer/winter solstice, wine trivia
- Select a country and have guests bring a bottle of wine from that country and perhaps a food item that will pair with that wine to share with others at the party.
- Select a grape varietal such as Cabernet Sauvignon. Each guest will bring a Cabernet to share from different countries / states. As host, you would decide either the country or states that provide Cabernet Sauvignon that guests would check off and let the host know what they are bringing in order to cover the highest number of areas. This event will allow guests to taste each of the wines and talk about which one was their favorite.

- Chefs / Cooks Challenge: identify a grocery store and note each aisle with food. Guests would choose a number and can only use ingredients from the aisle number they drew to make their dishes. They can also choose 1 protein to add to the food from their aisle. Of course you can plan a day for this event. Start by going to the grocery store and each guest or couple would shop for their food items from the chosen aisle. This event could be set up so that one guest/couple would take an afternoon appetizer or snack with a wine pairing for all involved. Couples can make appetizers, soup, salads, main course and the side dishes for the dinner and a dessert, of course all paired with wine! The specific course(s) and which guest(s)/couple will make the course must be made in advance of the visit to the store. This is a fun event and a chance to share cooking skills as well as their pairing skills.

Hosting a business dinner

When you are in business you may be expected to "entertain" clients. This is likely to include taking them to a restaurant for dinner. Because your company is picking up the tab for the dinner, oftentimes the clients are looking for you to order the drinks.

As you are probably aware, one of the first things out of the wait staff's mouth is "Can I start you off with a drink?" If the goal is to have drinks and socialize prior to ordering the food for the evening the following decisions must be made.

- If the clients prefer drinks other than wine, prior to dinner, you can determine the number of drinks that you would like to limit each client to and the length of time you plan on spending on the pre-dinner / socializing prior to having folks place their orders for dinner.
- If all or a portion of the clients will be drinking wine during the pre-dinner social, you should check with the wait staff to ask if they have a house wine, a happy hour or some other type of

discount program for drinks. This could be a substantial savings for the company not to mention that it can make you look good as well.

Now, back to the wine. It has been my experience that not all restaurants have a decent house wine. I have found that most of the whites are drinkable, especially the Pinot Grigio or Pinot Gris. But many of the red wines are all over the board and inconsistent. I would encourage clients to perhaps order the white wines if at all possible for the pre-dinner social (for those interested in wine). If you order red wine, please review the remainder of this chapter to help you with your decision.

Once you have made the decisions you can discretely talk to the wait staff and have them remind you when the designated time or number of drinks have been reached so they can help get the folks ready to order their meal.

I have also found during this social time many folks will talk about the menu and what they think they might order. If there is a lot of talk about appetizers, for example, you might begin the discussion with your party that you are going to place an order for a certain number of appetizers for everyone to share.

This is also a good time to talk with your wait staff and let them know that you are planning to order wines for the main course and you will order the wine after everyone has placed their order so you can find the best possible pairing. Certainly, if the restaurant has a wine steward or sommelier, you can ask for their advice. If you do, suggest that they show you the wine(s) recommended utilizing the menu (list) so that you can see the prices. This will help you stay within your budget.

If the restaurant does not have this individual, or you choose not to use them, you will need to determine which wine(s) to order.

Once it is decided what food items (main course) everyone has selected, you can better select the specific wines to pair with the meals. If needed, refer back to chapter 4 where you can find the specific dishes or something similar that will help you select the wines that will complement the meals.

Now it is time to select the wine from the restaurant's wine list. At this point you have selected your entrée and a wine to match.

As you look at the wine list, you are likely to observe one of the following:

- The wines may be listed by country. If so, find the country and grape variety you want. If that grape variety is not available from this country, look for it from another location.
- Sometimes the wines are listed by the grape variety, such as Pinot Grigio, Chardonnay, Pinot Noir, Cabernet Sauvignon, etc.
- The restaurant may organize the wines by body type. Usually that would be light bodied, medium bodied or full bodied. (See chapter 7 for more details on bodied wines.)

Once you notice how the wines are organized on the wine list, it will be easier for you to navigate and select the wine that will compliment your meal. Your work is done. All that is left is for you to enjoy your experience. If you are going to purchase one or more bottles how much you should pay for a wine is certainly based on what you want to spend. A good rule of thumb is that you may not want to purchase the least expensive wine from a particular category but you certainly do not have to purchase the most expensive bottle either unless of course, it is what you want.

Remember that each bottle of wine will likely provide 4-6 individual glasses of wine depending on the size of the pour. Typically that will be 4-6 ounces of wine per glass. This information can be found in more detail in the section *"Hosting a wine event"* earlier in this chapter.

Know that the majority of the restaurants mark up the wine prices as this is an area where the restaurant can help cover more of the overall costs. Knowing all of this, it has been my experience that there are many delightful wines in the middle range price category at restaurants. For an easy reference in the book, I discussed above how wines are often listed on a wine menu (list) and a little on pricing. This may be helpful to review occasionally.

CHAPTER 7

Going to a Restaurant

If the restaurant does not have a wine steward or sommelier, or you choose not to use them, you will need to determine which wine(s) to order.

Once you have decided on what food you are going to order, check chapter 4 in this book. Here you can find the specific dish or something similar that will tell you which wine variety to choose that will compliment your meal.

Now it is time to select the wine from the restaurant's wine list. At this point you have selected your entrée and a wine to match.

As you look at the wine list, you are likely to observe one of the following:

- The wines may be listed by country. If so, find the country and grape variety you want. If that grape variety is not available from this country, look for it from another location.
- Sometimes the wines are listed by the grape variety, such as Pinot Grigio, Chardonnay, Pinot Noir, Cabernet Sauvignon, etc.
- The restaurant may organize the wines by body type. Usually that would be light bodied, medium bodied or full bodied.

Once you notice how the wines are organized on the wine list, it will be easier for you to navigate and select the wine that will compliment your meal. Your work is done. All that is left is for you to enjoy your experience. If you are going to purchase one or more bottles how much you should pay for a wine is certainly based on what you want to spend. A good rule of thumb is that you may not want to purchase the least expensive wine from a particular category but you certainly do not have to purchase the most expensive bottle either unless of course, it is what you want.

Match light or delicate flavored foods with lighter bodied wines and full flavored foods with big-bodied wines. Examples:

Duck Frittes	Viognier,
Coq au vin	Dolcetto d'Alba
Chili	Dolcetto

Lighter bodied wines are like skim milk – lighter, more watery and they disappear quickly with little finish when you swallow. White examples: Riesling and Pinot Grigio. Red example: Beaujolais Village

The lighter body and dryness of a Pinot Gris from Alsace makes an excellent companion with a vegetable pizza with marinara sauce. You can also grill this pizza.

Medium bodied wines are like whole milk, they have much more flavor and hang in your mouth longer and linger once you swallow. White examples: Sauvignon Blanc, Arneis. Red examples: Some Merlot, Pinot Noir, Chianti, Some Syrah / Shiraz, Tempranillo

Medium to full bodied white wines - Chardonnay, Gavi, Bourdeaux Blanc, Viognier, White Burgundy. Foods that pair well with these wines include:

Smoked salmon, smoked seafood
Crab dip
Cheese fondue
Baked brie en croite / or plain brie
Gouda cheese
Scallops wrapped in bacon
Almost anything in a creamy or buttery sauce
Baba ganoush (eggplant spread)
Shrimp scampi

Grilled shrimp
Potato latkes
Guacamole / sliced avocado
All shellfish, seafood, chicken, turkey, duck
Muenster cheese
Swiss cheese

Light to medium bodied red wines
Pinot Noir, Beaujolais, Granache, some Merlots, Chianti
Baked stuffed mushrooms
Creamed mushroom bruschetta
Provolone cheese
Brie
Bacon
Ham (not salty)
Salmon (smoked or regular)
Sausage (not too spicy)
Hummus
Teriyaki chicken
Liver pate
Chicken livers wrapped in bacon

Full bodied wines are like whole cream – they have the most presence of all. Your mouth feels them the most and the flavor stays the longest. White examples: Chardonnay, White Burgundy. Red examples: Some Merlot, Cabernet Sauvignon, Zinfandel, Cabernet Franc, some Syrah / Shiraz, Bordeaux blends, Super Tuscans.

CHAPTER 8

Recipes

In this chapter you will find a few recipes along with a wine pairing. Try it at home with your family and friends.

Grilled Cedar Planked Salmon

Soak your cedar plank in water for at least 1 hour.

In this recipe I provide a rub for the salmon.

Rub:

1 teaspoon Bay Seasoning
1 teaspoon garlic powder
1 teaspoon ground cumin
1 ½ teaspoon of ground black pepper
1 teaspoon of sea salt (optional)
2 teaspoons of chili powder
1 tablespoon of smoked paprika
2 teaspoons of dry dill weed
1 teaspoon of coriander
1 ½ teaspoon Fennel seed
2 ½ tablespoons of brown sugar (light or regular)

Mix the rub spice in a mixing bowl and set aside.

Salmon

1 ½ to 2 pounds of salmon (cut in 4 equal pieces of 6 – 8 ounces each)
Brush salmon lightly on each side with olive oil.
Rub the spice mixture on the salmon with the desired amount of rub and set aside.

Preheat grill on low to medium – low heat.
Spray grill rack with non-stick spray.
Rub a small amount of olive oil on the cedar plank.
Place the salmon skin side down on the cedar plank.

Place the soaked plank and salmon on the pre-heated grill and close the lid. Grill for approximately 15-18 minutes or to desired level of doneness.

Remove the planked salmon from the grill.

Serve immediately.

As this will likely be the main dish for your meal, I recommend serving with Pinot Noir.

Coq Au Vin

2 Tablespoons Extra Virgin Olive Oil
4-5 Shallots
4 Chicken Breast (boneless)
1 Tablespoon Flour
¼ cup Brandy
1 Bottle Dry Red Wine*
1 sprig Thyme
3 cloves Garlic
8 ounces Mushrooms
4 sprigs Rosemary
Edible flowers
Risotto – see recipe within

Preheat oven to 325 degrees. In a skillet heat the oil over medium heat. Add the shallots and cook for about 10 minutes or until lightly browned. Add the chicken to a backing dish, salt and pepper to taste. Sprinkle the flour over the chicken. Heat the brandy in a small pan and pour it over the chicken. Using a long-handled match, light the brandy. When the flames subside, stir well to scrape the browned bits from the bottom of the pan. Add the shallots, wine, herbs (except the Rosemary) and garlic. Cover and bake for 1 hour.

Using a slotted spoon, transfer the chicken and shallots to a heated plate and cover with aluminum foil. Strain the liquids. Discard the solids. Return the liquid to the pan and cook over medium heat to reduce it by about one third. Return the chicken, shallots and mushrooms. Cook for about 10 minutes, uncovered. Serve over risotto.

Serving:
Put a serving size of the barley risotto in the center of a plate. Top with chicken. Stick a spring of rosemary into the chicken. Lay edible flowers on the plate.

* Recommend: Pinot Noir, Merlot or Cabernet Sauvignon. Pair the same with your meal.

Barley Risotto

1 cup Quick cooking Barley
2 cups Vegetable broth
1 small Onion, chopped
1 clove Garlic, finely chopped
1 Tablespoon of fresh parsley
8 ounces Mushroom
4 ounces Mozzarella cheese
¼ Teaspoon Pepper
Pinch Salt

Add barley to vegetable broth and bring to a boil. Lower the heat and simmer for 10 minutes or until barley is cooked and most of the water has been absorbed.

In the meantime, sauté the onion, mushroom, and garlic.

Add the onion, mushroom and garlic to the barley. Stir in the cheese until barley is creamy. Garnish with parsley.

Serve immediately.

Lasagna

½ pound Italian Sausage
½ pound Ground Beef
1 clove garlic, minced
1 tablespoon basil
1 ½ teaspoon salt
1 pound can Tomato
2 6-ounce cans Tomato Paste
1 package Lasagna noodles
2 eggs (or egg substitute)
3 cups Ricotta
½ cup Parmesan Cheese
2 tablespoons parsley
½ teaspoon pepper
1 package Mozzarella cheese
Pinch of salt

Brown meat; spoon off excess fat. Add the next 5 ingredients and simmer uncovered for 30 minutes, stirring occasionally. Cook noodles in large amount of boiling salted water until tender, drain and rinse.

Beat eggs and the remaining ingredients – except the mozzarella cheese.

Cover the bottom of the pan with a thin layer of sauce. Put down a layer of noodles then top with the Ricotta cheese mixture, parmesan cheese and mozzarella then sauce. Repeat layers.

Bake at 375 degrees about 30 minutes. Let stand 10 minutes before serving.

Variations: You can use your favorite store bought pasta sauce or you can omit the meat in the above recipe for a vegetarian version.

For a healthier dish you can substitute zucchini or eggplant for the noodles. Thinly cut into strips and layer. Substitute ground turkey for ground beef.

Recommended wine: Chianti, Sangiovese or Super Tuscan.

Pound Cake with Grilled Peaches

1 box of pound cake
1 bottle of peach wine
Peaches (1/2 the number of peaches for the number you will be servings)
Raspberries
Corn starch (for thickening)

Bake the pound cake according to package instructions. Substitute ½ of the water with peach wine.

Meanwhile, drop the peaches in boiling water for 40 seconds and then cool in an ice bath. Peel the peaches. Cut peaches in half. Grill until grill marks are visible. Remove from grill to cool.

Boil ½ cup of peach wine until reduced. Add in raspberries, continue to boil for 1 minute. Remove from heat and add ½ tablespoon of corn starch and stir until thickened.

Slice pound cake, top with half peach and serve with the raspberry-peach sauce.

I recommend serving with peach wine or Ice wine.

CHAPTER 9

Final Thoughts

Remember some of the following guidelines for wine and food pairings

- Drink Old World wines with Old World dishes. Old world wines come from Europe but can include other regions of the Mediterranean basin.
- New world wines refer to wines of the New World such as the United States, Australia, South America and South Africa.
- When ordering ethnic foods, if available, you can order wines from that country to pair with your meal. Examples include Rioja or Tempranillo with Spanish influenced dishes or Tuscan wines with Tuscan dishes. While this is not a necessity, typically the pairings are good and it might give you an opportunity to try a new wine.
- If a dish is made with a wine reduction or wine sauce, if unknown, ask what wine or grape varietal was used and order it with your meal or dessert.
- Fruits and some ingredients, such as barbeque sauces, and teriyaki sauces add sweetness to a dish. Carmelization that comes from roasting, grilling or sautéing can also contribute to the sweetness of a dish. Sweeter foods will likely decrease the perception of the sweetness of a wine. If the food has some sweetness, choose a wine that has a degree of sweetness as well. If it is a dessert and it is sweet, serve a dessert wine that is even sweeter.
- If you order a glass of wine at a restaurant and it does not taste right, ask the wait staff how long the bottle has been opened. More

times than not, the wine has probably sat open too long and was not properly sealed or perhaps the bottle was corked. In either case, you should be able to get a "fresh" glass of wine. In my experiences, the restaurant will open a new bottle. This will usually take care of the problem.

- Do not be afraid to ask if you can taste the wine before you order it. At most restaurants, especially if the particular wine of interest is sold by the glass as well as the bottle, you can receive a taste. This way you can see if the wine is what you thought.

Finally, I like to take a little time to discuss glassware (stemware). There are many folks, including myself, who feel that a better wine glass, specifically designed for a particular wine varietal can help you better enjoy the overall experience of the wine.

Especially when you are purchasing a nice wine for a special occasion at home or at a restaurant, a better glass can make a difference. Professional glass makers recognize that the shape of the glass can affect the taste of a wine. The specific shape and angle of the bowl affects your senses when you sniff and taste a wine. The tapered bowl helps concentrate the aromas of a wine. The shape and size of the bowl, as well as the diameter of the rim, affect the lift needed to deliver the wine to the mouth, changing where the wine is delivered to the tongue.

Grape varietal specific stemware, first discovered by Claus Riedel of Riedel Crystal in the 1950s, is responsible for the quality and intensity of the wines bouquet. It affects the texture of the wines by highlighting the variable mouth feel. It can highlight the flavor of a wine by creating a balanced interaction between fruit, minerality, acidity and the bitter components. It can enhance the finish by offering a pleasant, seamless, harmonious long lasting after taste.

There are so many other things we could talk about such as specifics on glassware (stemware), when to decanter a wine, aging of wine and vertical tastings. The list can go on and on. But these are other stories for another time or perhaps a future book.

So when you go to a restaurant, ask them if they have nicer glasses to serve the wine or they carry grape varietal stemware. Believe me, if you tried a side-by-side comparison of many restaurant regular stemware and the grape varietal specific stemware you could tell the difference. Unfortunately you may not always have this choice, but it never hurts to ask. Who knows, you may teach them a thing or two about stemware and they may purchase better stemware in the future.

Remember that people's palates are different. As such, even with all of this new knowledge and opportunity, there are times that you should drink what wines you like even if the pairings are not the most perfect. In the end, if it tastes good to you, then by all means order it!

I am happy that you chose to take this journey and learn more about wine as well as food and wine pairings. I hope you had some fun along the way.

As you become more knowledgeable and comfortable with wines. It is my hope that you continue to drink different wines and enjoy different pairings. While many folks have their favorite wines and perhaps food and wine pairings, it is always nice to expand your own horizon. Do not get in the same rut ordering at restaurant. With your new found knowledge you will be able to order or prepare many different meals with the confidence that you can select the right wine variety to pair with your food. This is especially important if you have any food ordering restrictions.

Finally – remember not to be intimidated. Have fun with your food and wine pairing! Ultimately drink what you want and what you like.

Cheers!

Made in United States
Orlando, FL
10 February 2024

43521186R10054